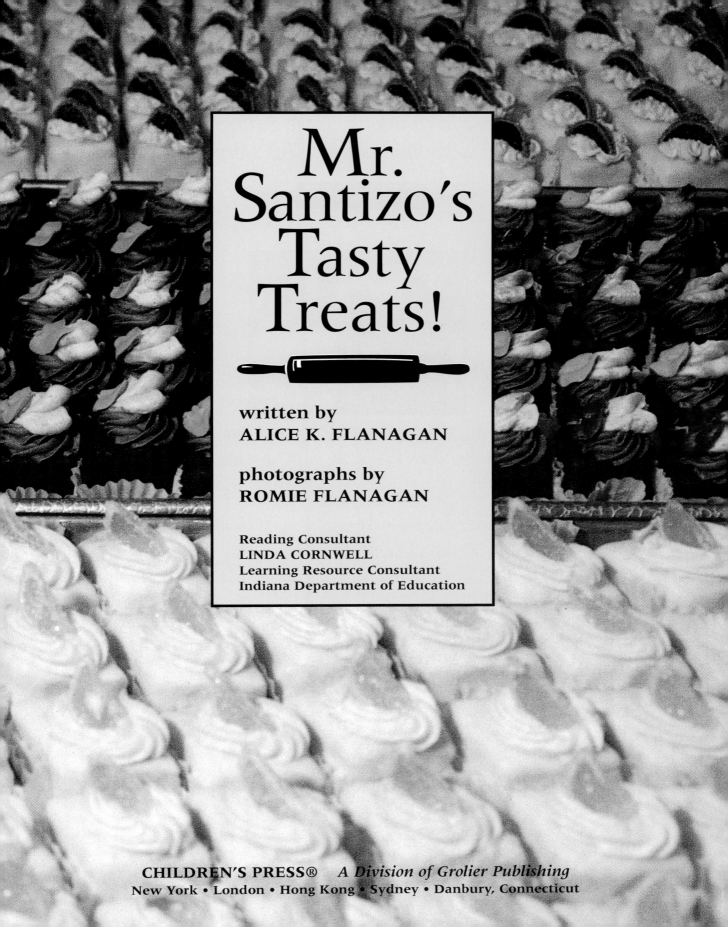

Mr. Santizo's Tasty Treats!

written by
ALICE K. FLANAGAN

photographs by
ROMIE FLANAGAN

Reading Consultant
LINDA CORNWELL
Learning Resource Consultant
Indiana Department of Education

CHILDREN'S PRESS®   *A Division of Grolier Publishing*
New York • London • Hong Kong • Sydney • Danbury, Connecticut

Special thanks to Jorge Santizo
for allowing us to tell his story.

Also thanks to the Stanton Family. Without
them, this book would not have been made.

Author's Note:
Mr. Santizo's last name is pronounced san-TEE-zoh.

Library of Congress Cataloging-in-Publication Data
Flanagan, Alice.
    Mr. Santizo's tasty treats! / written by Alice K. Flanagan ; photographs
by Romie Flanagan ; reading consultant, Linda Cornwell.
        p.   cm. — (Our neighborhood)
    Summary: Text and photographs follow the activities of a Guatemalan
American who works making cakes, breads, and other baked goods in a
neighborhood bakery.
    ISBN 0-516-20771-7 (lib.bdg.)   0-516-26296-3 (pbk.)
    1. Baking—Juvenile literature. [1. Bakers and bakeries. 2. Occupa-
tions.] I. Flanagan, Romie, ill. II. Title. III. Series: Our neighborhood
(New York, N.Y.)
    TX681.F53   1998
    664'.752—dc21

                                                              97-16399
                                                                 CIP
                                                                  AC

Photographs ©: Romie Flanagan

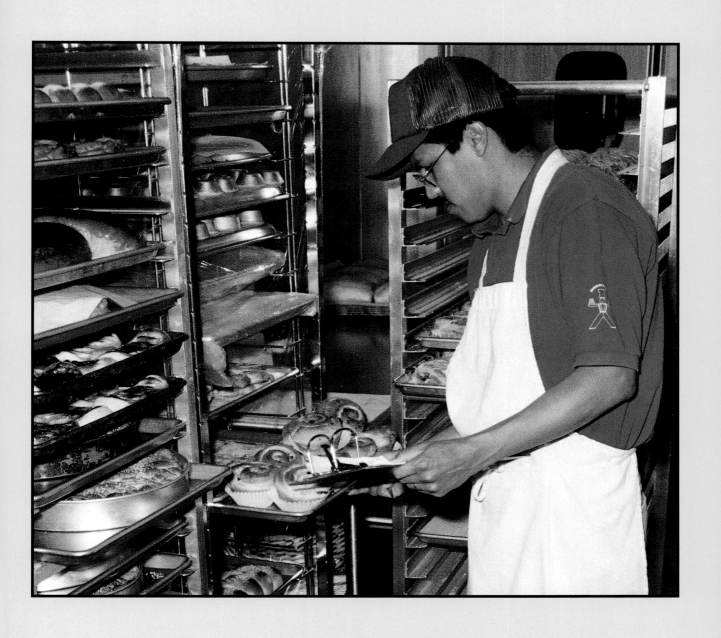

Can you smell the hot bread baking and the fresh cookies and apple cakes?

Would you like to taste one of the treats that Mr. Santizo makes?

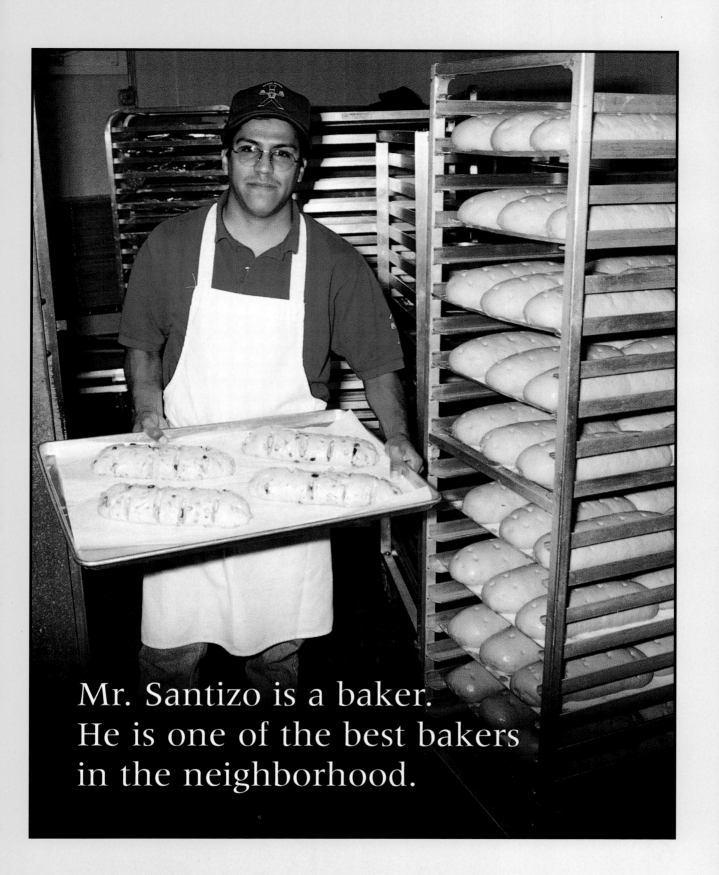

Mr. Santizo is a baker.
He is one of the best bakers
in the neighborhood.

About fifteen years ago, Mr. Santizo and his wife moved to the United States from Guatemala.

Mr. Santizo took a job washing dishes during the day. At night, he trained to be a baker.

Now the Santizos have three children.
They are very proud of them.

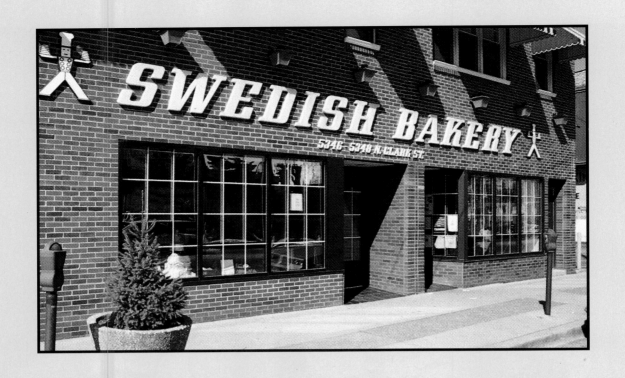

Mr. Santizo works in this bakery.

He is in charge of making the baked
goods in the store—everything from
doughnuts and cookies to breads
and coffee cakes.

Each morning, Mr. Santizo and the head baker check the orders that must be filled that day.

Mr. Santizo makes sure all of the workers have the ingredients and kitchen tools they need to fill the orders.

Mr. Santizo fills the special orders himself.

He makes the cakes and breads that customers order for birthdays, weddings, and special events.

Usually, Mr. Santizo follows a recipe when he bakes. The recipe tells him what to mix together and how much to use.

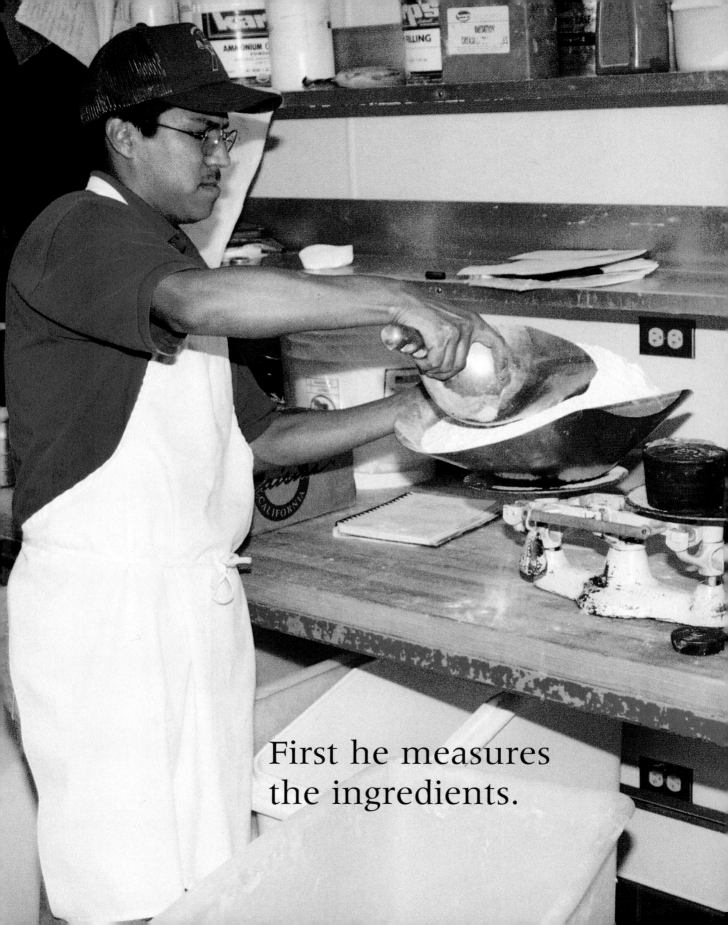

First he measures
the ingredients.

Then he mixes them very well.

Mr. Santizo is very careful when he uses the fast-moving machines,

the sharp knives,

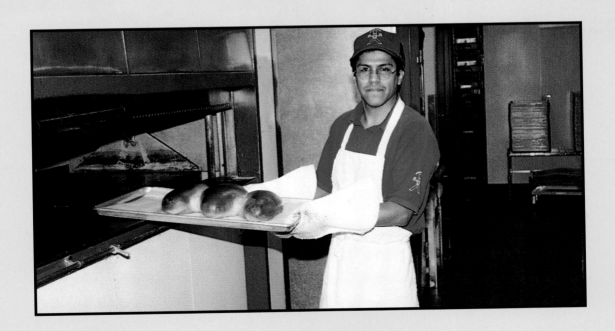

and the hot ovens.

After he bakes and frosts a cake,

18

it's ready to be decorated.

For birthday cakes, Mr. Santizo
chooses bright, happy colors.

Around each cake, he sprinkles tiny
pieces of candy.

Then, with steady hands, he makes candy flowers . . .

and writes a birthday greeting.

Toy balloons add the final touch to a beautiful birthday cake!

Just like an artist, Mr. Santizo creates
and decorates wedding cakes.

He tries to please his customers by making what they want.

Mr. Santizo feels proud when
customers tell him that they like
his work.

And he listens when they tell him they would like him to make something different for them.

Mr. Santizo likes his job. He does it very well. You can be sure that whatever he makes, it is his very best.

Ask an adult to help you make Mr. Santizo's special chocolate chip pecan cookies!

(This recipe will make about 100 small cookies.)

1. In a large bowl, put 1 pound softened butter (4 sticks) and 2 cups of brown sugar. Mix until creamy.

2. Add 4 large eggs and mix well.

3. Add ½ teaspoon of vanilla and mix well.

4. In another large bowl, put 4 cups of flour and ¼ teaspoon of salt.

5. Slowly add the flour and salt to the butter, sugar, eggs, and vanilla, mixing well.

6. Add a 12-ounce package of chocolate chips and a 12-ounce package of pecans. Mix.

7. Make 1-inch size balls and place them on an ungreased cookie sheet.

8. Bake in the oven at 350° for 8 to 10 minutes.

Meet the Author
and the Photographer

Alice and Romie Flanagan live in Chicago, Illinois, and have been involved in publishing for many years. Alice is a writer, and Romie is a photographer. As husband and wife, they enjoy working together closely. They hope their books help children learn about the people in their community and how their jobs affect the neighborhood.